Ultimate Survival Guide

Master Essential Skills and Techniques for Any Disaster

Abe Loxley

Ultimate Survival Guide

© Copyright 2024 by **Abe Loxley**

All rights reserved

This document is geared towards providing exact and reliable information with regards to the topic and issue covered. The publication is sold with the idea that the publisher is not required to render accounting, officially permitted, or otherwise, qualified services. If advice is necessary, legal or professional, a practiced individual in the profession should be ordered.

From a Declaration of Principles which was accepted and approved equally by a Committee of the American Bar Association and a Committee of Publishers and Associations.

In no way is it legal to reproduce, duplicate, or transmit any part of this document in either electronic means or in printed format. Recording of this publication is strictly prohibited and any storage of this document is not allowed unless with written permission from the publisher. All rights reserved.

The information provided herein is stated to be truthful and consistent, in that any liability, in terms of inattention or otherwise, by any usage or abuse of any policies, processes, or directions contained within is the solitary and utter responsibility of the recipient reader. Under no circumstances will any legal responsibility or blame be held against the publisher for any reparation, damages, or monetary loss due to the information herein, either directly or indirectly.

Respective authors own all copyrights not held by the publisher.

The information herein is offered for informational purposes solely, and is universal as so. The presentation of the information is without contract or any type of guarantee assurance.

The trademarks that are used are without any consent, and the publication of the trademark is without permission or backing by the trademark owner. All trademarks and brands within this book are for clarifying purposes only and are owned by the owners themselves, not affiliated with this document.

TABLE OF CONTENTS

Chapter 1: Introduction to Survivalism 4
What is Survivalism? 4
The Importance of Preparedness 9
The Survival Mindset 14
Basic Principles of Survival 19
Overview of Key Survival Skills 24

Chapter 2: Building a Survival Kit 30
Essential Items for Any Kit 30
Customizing Your Kit for Different Scenarios 35
Budget-Friendly Survival Kits 40
Maintaining and Updating Your Kit 45
Portable vs. Staticnary Kits 49

Chapter 3: Water Procurement and Purification 54
Finding Water Sources 54
Purification Methods 59
Long-Term Water Storage 64
Building a Rainwater Collection System 68
DIY Water Filters 73

Chapter 4: Food Acquisition and Preservation 78
Foraging for Edible Plants 78
Hunting and Trapping 83
Fishing Techniques 89
Food Preservation Methods 95
Building a Food Storage System 101

Chapter 1: Introduction to Survivalism

What is Survivalism?

Survivalism is a philosophy and a way of life grounded in the belief that individuals and communities should be prepared to endure and thrive through any number of potential crises. This mindset is not born out of paranoia but from a pragmatic understanding of the world's inherent unpredictability. From natural disasters to economic collapse, the survivalist seeks to be resilient in the face of adversity, ensuring that they have the skills, resources, and mental fortitude to survive when conventional support systems fail.

At its core, survivalism is about self-reliance. The modern world encourages dependency on complex supply chains and societal structures. While this system provides convenience, it also creates vulnerability. A survivalist recognizes this fragility and takes proactive steps to mitigate risks. This involves developing a diverse set of skills, accumulating necessary supplies, and cultivating a mindset that prioritizes adaptability and problem-solving.

The importance of preparedness cannot be overstated. In times of crisis, those who are unprepared often find themselves at the mercy of circumstances beyond their control. A well-prepared individual, however, will have the tools and knowledge to navigate these challenges effectively. This preparedness spans various domains, including physical supplies, knowledge, and mental readiness.

A crucial aspect of survivalism is the survival mindset. This mindset is characterized by a blend of optimism, realism, and a relentless will to persevere. Optimism fuels the belief that solutions are possible and that challenges can be overcome. Realism grounds this optimism in a clear-eyed assessment of potential threats and the steps needed to mitigate them. The will to persevere is the driving force that keeps a survivalist moving forward, even in the face of daunting obstacles.

Basic principles of survival guide the actions and decisions of a survivalist. These principles include the rule of threes, which states that a person can survive three minutes without air, three hours without shelter in extreme conditions, three days without water, and three weeks without food. These guidelines help prioritize actions in an emergency. Additionally, the principles of conservation and resourcefulness underscore the importance of making the most of available resources and minimizing waste.

Key survival skills are essential to putting these principles into practice. These skills range from basic first aid and fire-starting to more advanced techniques like navigation, sustainable food procurement, and water purification. Each skill contributes to a survivalist's ability to remain self-sufficient and resilient in various scenarios. For instance, knowing how to build a shelter can protect against harsh weather, while proficiency in first aid can prevent minor injuries from becoming life-threatening.

Survivalism also emphasizes the importance of community. While self-reliance is a cornerstone of the philosophy, no individual is an island. Building a network of like-minded individuals can provide mutual support and shared resources. In a crisis, a well-coordinated group can achieve much more than an isolated individual. This sense of community extends to knowledge-sharing, where experienced survivalists mentor and educate newcomers, fostering a culture of preparedness and resilience.

In practice, survivalism involves continuous learning and adaptation. The world is constantly changing, and new threats can emerge without warning. Staying informed about potential risks and updating one's skills and supplies accordingly is crucial. This proactive approach ensures that a survivalist remains prepared for a wide range of scenarios, from natural disasters like earthquakes and hurricanes to human-made crises such as economic downturns or civil unrest.

A survivalist's journey often begins with a shift in perspective. Rather than viewing preparedness as a daunting task, it becomes a rewarding pursuit. The process of learning new skills and acquiring essential knowledge can be empowering, instilling a sense of confidence and security. This journey is unique to each individual, shaped by personal circumstances, geographic location, and specific concerns.

For many, the initial steps into survivalism involve assessing current levels of preparedness and identifying areas for improvement. This might mean creating a basic emergency kit, learning how to purify water, or developing a family communication plan. Over time, these initial steps evolve into a comprehensive preparedness strategy, encompassing everything from long-term food storage to advanced survival techniques.

The practical benefits of survivalism extend beyond crisis situations. Many survival skills, such as gardening, home repair, and first aid, are valuable in everyday life. These skills contribute to a more self-sufficient and sustainable lifestyle, reducing reliance on external systems and fostering a deeper connection with the natural world. Moreover, the confidence gained from being prepared can enhance overall well-being, reducing anxiety about potential disruptions and increasing resilience in the face of everyday challenges.

Survivalism is not just about individual readiness but also about fostering a culture of preparedness. This culture encourages critical thinking, self-sufficiency, and mutual support. By promoting these values, survivalism contributes to more resilient communities and a more robust society. Preparedness becomes a shared responsibility, with individuals and groups working together to ensure collective security and well-being.

The journey of a survivalist is ongoing, marked by continuous learning and adaptation. As new information and technologies emerge, survivalists integrate these advancements into their preparedness strategies. This dynamic approach ensures that they remain equipped to handle both current and future challenges. By staying vigilant and proactive, survivalists embody a spirit of resilience that is essential in an unpredictable world.

In essence, survivalism is about cultivating a mindset and lifestyle that prioritize preparedness, self-reliance, and resilience. It is a proactive response to the inherent uncertainties of life, grounded in practical skills and a strong sense of community. Through continuous learning and adaptation, survivalists strive to be ready for anything, ensuring their ability to thrive no matter what the future holds.

The Importance of Preparedness

Preparedness is the cornerstone of survival. It is the proactive approach to mitigating potential risks and ensuring that you and your loved ones can navigate through crises with minimal disruption. In a world where natural disasters, economic instability, and unforeseen emergencies are becoming more commonplace, being prepared is not just a precaution but a necessity. It transforms the uncertainty of the future into manageable scenarios, where you have the tools and knowledge to maintain safety and well-being.

Imagine the sudden onset of a natural disaster, such as a hurricane or earthquake. Without prior preparation, the immediate response is often panic, followed by a scramble for essential supplies that may no longer be available. Conversely, those who have taken the time to prepare can act swiftly and efficiently, following a predetermined plan. This not only increases the chances of survival but also reduces stress and anxiety during the event. Preparedness offers a sense of control in situations that are otherwise chaotic and unpredictable.

Consider the aftermath of a natural disaster. In many cases, it can take days or even weeks for emergency services to reach affected areas. During this period, having a stockpile of food, water, and medical supplies can be the difference between life and death. Basic necessities such as clean water and non-perishable food items can sustain you until help arrives or normalcy is restored. Moreover, having a well-thought-out emergency plan ensures that every member of your household knows what to do and where to go, further enhancing your collective resilience.

Preparedness is not limited to physical supplies. It also encompasses the acquisition of skills and knowledge that can be invaluable in an emergency. For instance, knowing how to perform basic first aid, start a fire, or purify water are critical skills that can significantly improve your chances of survival. These skills provide a buffer against the vulnerabilities that arise when external support systems fail. They empower you to take action and solve problems independently, fostering a sense of self-reliance.

Financial preparedness is another crucial aspect. Economic downturns and personal financial crises can strike unexpectedly, leaving you vulnerable if you are not prepared. Maintaining an emergency fund can help cushion the blow of sudden expenses such as medical bills, car repairs, or job loss. This financial buffer allows you to navigate through tough times without resorting to high-interest loans or falling into debt. Additionally, understanding basic financial principles and having a budget in place can help you manage your resources more effectively, ensuring long-term stability.

Mental preparedness is equally important. In high-stress situations, a calm and focused mind can make the difference between making a life-saving decision and succumbing to panic. Mental resilience is built through regular practice and exposure to challenging scenarios. This can be achieved through activities such as emergency drills, meditation, and stress management techniques. By training your mind to remain calm and focused, you enhance your ability to think clearly and act decisively in emergencies.

Community preparedness is another vital component. While individual readiness is essential, the collective preparedness of a community can significantly amplify the effectiveness of any response to a crisis. Strong community ties and mutual support networks can provide additional resources and assistance that may not be available to individuals acting alone. Organizing community preparedness workshops, sharing resources, and establishing communication plans are ways to foster a resilient community. When disaster strikes, a well-prepared community can mobilize quickly, provide support to its members, and ensure a more effective recovery.

Preparedness also involves staying informed about potential threats and understanding the specific risks associated with your location. This includes being aware of natural hazards such as floods, wildfires, or tornadoes, as well as human-made threats like industrial accidents or civil unrest. By staying informed, you can tailor your preparedness efforts to address the most likely scenarios, ensuring that your resources and skills are aligned with the risks you face.

One practical step in preparedness is creating a comprehensive emergency plan. This plan should outline the actions to take in various scenarios, contact information for family members and emergency services, and designated meeting points. It should be reviewed and practiced regularly to ensure that everyone involved is familiar with the procedures. An effective emergency plan reduces confusion and ensures that everyone knows their role, which can be critical in a high-pressure situation.

Regularly updating and maintaining your preparedness efforts is also crucial. Supplies can expire, skills can become rusty, and new threats can emerge. Setting a schedule to review and refresh your emergency supplies, update your emergency plan, and practice essential skills ensures that your preparedness efforts remain effective. This continuous process of evaluation and improvement keeps you ready to face any new challenges that may arise.

Preparedness extends beyond immediate survival. It encompasses long-term strategies for maintaining self-sufficiency and resilience. This includes considerations such as sustainable living practices, self-defense, and long-term food storage. By incorporating these elements into your preparedness efforts, you build a foundation that supports not just survival but also the ability to thrive in adverse conditions.

The importance of preparedness is underscored by the fact that crises often occur without warning. Whether it is a sudden natural disaster, an economic collapse, or a personal emergency, being unprepared can lead to devastating consequences. Conversely, those who have invested time and effort into preparedness can navigate these challenges with confidence and competence. They are not only equipped to survive but to support others and contribute to the recovery process.

In summary, preparedness is a multifaceted approach that encompasses physical supplies, skills, financial stability, mental resilience, and community support. It transforms uncertainty into manageable scenarios and provides a sense of control in the face of chaos. By prioritizing preparedness, you enhance your ability to protect yourself and your loved ones, ensuring that you are ready to face whatever challenges the future may hold.

The Survival Mindset

Developing a survival mindset is the foundation of effective preparedness. It's a blend of mental resilience, adaptability, and an unwavering determination to overcome adversity. Unlike physical skills and supplies, which can be accumulated and stored, the survival mindset is cultivated through experience, practice, and a conscious effort to reshape how you perceive and respond to challenges. This mindset transforms theoretical preparedness into practical, actionable responses during crises.

Imagine finding yourself lost in a dense forest with nightfall approaching. Panic is a natural initial reaction, but it's your mindset that will determine your next steps. A survival mindset shifts your focus from fear to problem-solving. Instead of succumbing to panic, you start assessing your surroundings, identifying resources, and formulating a plan to either find your way back or create a temporary shelter for the night. This ability to remain calm and think clearly under pressure is a hallmark of the survival mindset.

Adaptability is a key component. In any emergency, conditions can change rapidly, and rigid plans often fail. A survival mindset embraces flexibility, understanding that the best-laid plans may need to be adjusted on the fly. This means being open to new information, willing to change course, and constantly reassessing the situation. For example, if your initial plan to find a water source fails, you must quickly pivot to alternative strategies without becoming disheartened.

Mental resilience, or the ability to withstand and recover from stress, is another crucial element. This resilience is built over time through exposure to challenging situations, both real and simulated. Regularly participating in activities that push your limits, such as rigorous physical training, survival drills, or even high-pressure work environments, can enhance your mental toughness. These experiences teach you to manage stress, maintain focus, and make sound decisions even when under extreme pressure.

Visualization is a powerful tool for developing a survival mindset. By mentally rehearsing different emergency scenarios, you can prepare your mind for the real thing. Visualization helps you anticipate potential problems and practice your responses in a safe, controlled environment. For instance, imagine a scenario where you need to evacuate your home quickly. Visualize each step: gathering your emergency kit, ensuring family members are safe, and navigating to your predetermined safe location. This mental practice makes the actual event less overwhelming and more manageable.

Another aspect of the survival mindset is the ability to prioritize effectively. In any crisis, there are countless tasks that need attention, but not all are equally important. The ability to identify and focus on the most critical tasks first is vital. This often involves the "rule of threes" in survival: humans can survive three minutes without air, three hours without shelter in extreme conditions, three days without water, and three weeks without food. This guideline helps prioritize actions in a survival situation, ensuring that the most immediate threats are addressed first.

Maintaining a positive attitude is essential. While it may seem cliché, a positive outlook can significantly impact your ability to survive. Optimism fuels determination and persistence, helping you push through difficult times. It's not about ignoring the gravity of the situation but rather focusing on the belief that you can find solutions and overcome obstacles. This positive mindset can keep morale high, both for yourself and for any group you might be leading or supporting.

Self-awareness is also critical. Understanding your strengths and weaknesses allows you to make better decisions in a crisis. It helps you leverage your skills effectively and seek help in areas where you might be lacking. Regular self-assessment and honest reflection can enhance this self-awareness, making you a more effective and reliable individual in survival situations.

Resourcefulness, the ability to make do with what is available, is a skill honed through a survival mindset. It involves creative problem-solving and the ability to see potential uses for items beyond their intended purpose. For example, in a survival scenario, a plastic bottle can be transformed into a water filter, a signaling device, or even a container for boiling water. Practicing resourcefulness in everyday life can prepare you to think outside the box when conventional solutions are unavailable.

Leadership, even on a small scale, is an integral part of the survival mindset. Whether you are leading a family, a group of friends, or even just yourself, having the ability to make decisions, delegate tasks, and maintain cohesion is crucial. Good leaders remain calm, inspire confidence, and keep the group focused on common goals. Leadership skills can be developed through practice, training, and observing effective leaders in action.

Preparedness also involves continuous learning and skill development. The world is constantly changing, and new challenges can arise unexpectedly. Staying informed about potential threats, learning new skills, and keeping up with advancements in survival techniques ensure you remain prepared for a wide range of scenarios. This commitment to lifelong learning reinforces the survival mindset, making you more adaptable and resilient.

Lastly, the survival mindset includes a strong sense of purpose. This purpose can be as broad as the will to live or as specific as the desire to protect loved ones. Having a clear purpose provides motivation and direction, helping you stay focused and driven during challenging times. It gives meaning to your actions and decisions, fueling your determination to overcome obstacles and achieve your survival goals.

Developing a survival mindset is a continuous process, requiring dedication and effort. It involves reshaping how you think, react, and adapt to challenges. By cultivating mental resilience, adaptability, positivity, resourcefulness, and a sense of purpose, you can enhance your ability to navigate crises effectively. This mindset not only prepares you for emergencies but also enriches your everyday life, making you more capable, confident, and resilient in the face of any challenge.

Basic Principles of Survival

Survival can often hinge on a few fundamental principles that, if understood and applied, greatly enhance your chances of making it through an emergency. These principles are rooted in simplicity and practical wisdom, designed to guide your actions and decisions when faced with the unpredictable and often harsh realities of survival situations.

First and foremost, the principle of staying calm cannot be overstated. Panic is a natural response to danger, but it can cloud your judgment and lead to poor decision-making. The ability to remain calm and composed allows you to assess your situation accurately and make rational choices. This calmness can be cultivated through regular practice of mindfulness, meditation, or simply through repetitive exposure to stressful situations in a controlled environment. By training your mind to stay calm, you maintain a clear head, which is crucial for survival.

Next is the principle of situational awareness. This involves being acutely aware of your surroundings and understanding the context of your environment. Whether you're in an urban setting during a disaster or lost in the wilderness, knowing your immediate environment helps you identify potential threats and resources. Practice this by always taking a moment to observe and understand your surroundings when you enter a new area.

Note the location of exits, sources of water, potential shelters, and any hazards. This habit can become second nature and significantly improve your ability to react appropriately in an emergency.

The principle of prioritization is essential. In any survival scenario, you must prioritize your actions based on immediate needs. The "rule of threes" is a useful guideline: you can survive three minutes without air, three hours without shelter in extreme conditions, three days without water, and three weeks without food. This hierarchy helps you focus on what is most critical first. For example, if you find yourself in freezing conditions, securing shelter and warmth becomes your top priority before seeking water or food.

Resourcefulness is another key principle. Survival often requires making do with what you have or can find. This means being creative and thinking outside the box. For instance, a simple plastic bag can serve multiple purposes: collecting water, acting as a makeshift poncho, or insulating your feet. Regularly challenge yourself to find multiple uses for everyday items to develop this resourceful mindset. This ability to improvise can be a lifesaver when conventional resources are unavailable.

Building and maintaining a fire is a fundamental survival skill that encompasses several principles: warmth, signaling, and water purification. Fire provides heat, which is crucial for preventing hypothermia, especially in cold environments. It also acts as a signal for rescuers and can be used to purify water, making it safe to drink. Practice making a fire in various conditions to ensure you can do it efficiently when it matters most. Learn different methods, such as using a fire starter, friction-based techniques, or even focusing sunlight with a magnifying glass.

Shelter is another cornerstone of survival. It protects you from the elements, whether it's rain, wind, snow, or the scorching sun. A well-constructed shelter helps maintain your body's core temperature, which is vital for survival. When building a shelter, consider location, materials, and design. Use natural features like rock overhangs or fallen trees, and insulate with leaves, branches, and other materials. Regularly practicing shelter-building in different environments can help you quickly create effective protection when needed.

Water is essential for life, and finding and purifying it is a crucial survival principle. Dehydration can set in quickly, impairing your physical and mental functions. Learn to identify natural water sources such as streams, rivers, and lakes. Understand methods of water purification, including boiling, filtration, and chemical treatments. Carrying a portable water filter or purification tablets in your survival kit can provide a reliable way to ensure you have safe drinking water. Additionally, knowing how to collect rainwater or dew can be invaluable in areas where natural bodies of water are scarce.

Food, while not as immediately critical as water or shelter, is still an important aspect of survival. Knowing how to source food from your environment can sustain you over longer periods. This includes foraging for edible plants, trapping small animals, fishing, and even insect consumption. Educate yourself on the local flora and fauna of the areas you frequent, learning which plants are safe to eat and how to catch or trap animals. Skills such as setting snares, fishing, and basic hunting can provide essential nutrition when other food sources are unavailable.

Another principle is the importance of signaling for rescue. In many survival situations, the ultimate goal is to be found and rescued. This means knowing how to signal effectively to attract the attention of rescuers. Fire, mirrors, whistles, bright clothing, and even creating large ground signals using rocks or logs can increase your visibility. Understanding international distress signals, such as three fires in a triangle or three blasts of a whistle, can also improve your chances of being located.

The principle of first aid is also critical. Injuries can occur at any time, and knowing basic first aid can prevent minor issues from becoming life-threatening. Learn how to treat wounds, fractures, burns, and other common injuries. Carry a well-stocked first aid kit and ensure you know how to use all of its contents. Regularly taking first aid courses can keep your knowledge up to date and your skills sharp.

Lastly, the principle of mental resilience is vital. Survival is as much a mental challenge as it is a physical one. Maintaining a positive attitude, setting small achievable goals, and keeping your mind occupied can prevent despair and maintain morale. Techniques such as visualization, where you imagine successfully navigating through your challenges, can bolster your mental strength. Building this resilience through regular mental exercises and maintaining a strong sense of purpose can be the difference between giving up and surviving.

Understanding and internalizing these basic principles of survival equips you with a strong foundation to face emergencies. Whether you're dealing with natural disasters, getting lost in the wilderness, or facing any other crisis, these principles guide your actions and decisions, increasing your chances of survival and eventual rescue. Consistent practice and preparation ensure these principles become second nature, ready to be called upon when needed most.

Overview of Key Survival Skills

Survival skills form the bedrock of your ability to endure and thrive in emergency situations. These skills, honed through knowledge and practice, are essential when you find yourself in unexpected and potentially life-threatening scenarios. Understanding and mastering these key survival skills can make the difference between life and death, and they provide a solid foundation for any survival plan.

Navigating your environment is a critical skill, whether you are in urban chaos or deep wilderness. Being able to orient yourself and find your way to safety or resources is paramount. Traditional navigation skills, such as using a map and compass, remain invaluable. Learning to read topographical maps and understanding how to use a compass can guide you even when technology fails. Additionally, natural navigation techniques, like using the position of the sun and stars, can help you determine direction. For example, the North Star, Polaris, is a reliable indicator of north in the Northern Hemisphere.

Building a fire is among the most essential survival skills. Fire provides warmth, light, and a means to cook food and purify water. It also serves as a signal for rescuers. Mastering the art of fire-making involves knowing multiple methods, such as using matches, lighters, fire starters, and friction-based techniques like the bow drill. Practice making fire under various conditions, including wet and windy environments, to ensure you can create and maintain a fire when needed. Gather tinder, kindling, and fuel in advance, and understand the principles of building a fire that will sustain itself.

Finding and purifying water is another crucial skill. The human body can only survive a few days without water, making it imperative to locate and treat water sources. Learn to identify natural water sources such as streams, rivers, and lakes. However, not all water is safe to drink directly. Techniques for purifying water include boiling, using chemical tablets, and filtering. Boiling is the most reliable method, as it kills pathogens effectively. Carrying a portable water filter or purification tablets in your survival kit ensures you have a backup plan for safe drinking water.

Shelter construction is vital for protection against the elements. Exposure to extreme weather can lead to hypothermia or heatstroke, both of which are life-threatening. Learn to build various types of shelters using natural materials or items you have on hand. In cold environments, constructing a debris hut or a snow cave can provide insulation and warmth. In hot climates, creating shade with a simple lean-to using branches and leaves can prevent overheating. Regularly practicing shelter-building ensures you can quickly and effectively create a safe haven when necessary.

First aid knowledge is indispensable in survival situations. Injuries can occur at any time, and knowing how to treat wounds, fractures, burns, and other common injuries can prevent complications and save lives. Enroll in a comprehensive first aid course to learn these skills. Familiarize yourself with the contents of a first aid kit and understand how to use each item. For example, knowing how to clean and dress a wound, splint a broken bone, and perform CPR can be crucial in emergencies. Regularly check and replenish your first aid kit to ensure it is always ready for use.

Food procurement is essential for long-term survival. While humans can survive for weeks without food, lack of nutrition will eventually lead to weakness and impaired cognitive function. Learn to identify edible plants, insects, and animals in your environment. Foraging for wild edibles requires knowledge of local flora, so study field guides and take courses on plant identification. Trapping and fishing are also effective ways to secure food. Practice setting snares and fishing with simple equipment to increase your chances of obtaining sustenance.

Signaling for help is a critical skill in ensuring rescue. Whether you are lost in the wilderness or trapped in an urban disaster, being able to attract the attention of rescuers can save your life. Understand how to use mirrors, whistles, and fire to create signals. Building large ground signals with rocks or logs can be seen from the air. Learning international distress signals, such as three fires in a triangle or three whistle blasts, can increase your visibility to rescuers. Carrying a signaling device like a whistle or mirror in your kit ensures you can call for help when needed.

Tool and weapon crafting can be essential for survival. When modern tools are unavailable, the ability to create implements from natural materials can aid in building shelter, procuring food, and defending yourself. Learn to craft basic tools such as knives, spears, and fishing hooks using stones, bones, and wood. Understanding how to shape and sharpen these materials increases their effectiveness. Practice these skills regularly to ensure you can create reliable tools in a survival situation.

Mental resilience is perhaps the most important survival skill. The ability to stay calm, focused, and positive can greatly influence your chances of survival. Developing mental toughness involves training your mind to handle stress and adversity. Techniques such as meditation, visualization, and controlled exposure to challenging situations can build resilience. Setting small, achievable goals and maintaining a sense of purpose can keep you motivated. Remember, the mind can be your greatest ally or your worst enemy in survival scenarios.

Resourcefulness and adaptability are key to overcoming unexpected challenges. The ability to improvise and make use of available materials can provide solutions to problems you might face. Practice thinking creatively and finding multiple uses for everyday items. For instance, a plastic bottle can be used to collect water, start a fire with a lens, or create a makeshift lantern. Cultivating this mindset of resourcefulness ensures you are prepared to handle unforeseen circumstances.

Effective communication is crucial, especially when you are in a group. Clear and concise communication can prevent misunderstandings and ensure everyone knows their roles and responsibilities. Learn to use hand signals and other non-verbal forms of communication if verbal communication is not possible. Establishing a chain of command and regular check-ins can keep the group organized and focused on survival tasks.

Lastly, continuous learning and practice are essential to maintaining your survival skills. The world is constantly changing, and new challenges can emerge. Stay informed about the latest survival techniques and advancements. Participate in survival courses, read books, and practice your skills regularly. This commitment to ongoing education ensures you remain prepared and adaptable in any situation.

Mastering these key survival skills provides a comprehensive toolkit for facing emergencies. Whether you are navigating unfamiliar terrain, building a fire, finding water, constructing shelter, administering first aid, procuring food, signaling for help, crafting tools, maintaining mental resilience, being resourceful, communicating effectively, or continuously learning, these skills form the foundation of your survival strategy. Consistent practice and dedication to improving these abilities ensure you are ready to face any challenge that comes your way.

Chapter 2: Building a Survival Kit

Essential Items for Any Kit

A well-prepared survival kit is the cornerstone of any effective emergency plan. Having the right tools and supplies can make the difference between safety and peril, providing the necessary resources to handle unexpected situations. Crafting a comprehensive kit requires thoughtful consideration of your environment, potential risks, and personal needs. This chapter will guide you through the essential items every survival kit should contain, ensuring you are equipped to face a variety of emergencies.

First and foremost, a reliable source of clean water is paramount. Dehydration can set in quickly, impairing your ability to think and act clearly. Your kit should include a minimum of one liter of water per person per day, ideally enough to last three days. While bottled water is convenient, consider including a portable water filter or purification tablets. These tools allow you to treat water from natural sources, extending your supply and ensuring you have access to safe drinking water in any situation. A collapsible water container is a valuable addition, as it can be easily stored and filled as necessary.

Equally important is a means to start a fire. Fire provides warmth, light, and a way to cook food and purify water. It can also serve as a signal for rescuers. Include multiple fire-starting methods in your kit, such as waterproof matches, a lighter, and a magnesium fire starter. Ensure you have a supply of tinder, such as cotton balls soaked in petroleum jelly or commercial fire starters, to help ignite your fire quickly. Practicing fire-making techniques before an emergency arises will increase your confidence and proficiency in using these tools.

Food is another critical component of your survival kit. While the human body can survive for several weeks without food, lack of nutrition will eventually lead to weakness and impaired cognitive function. Pack non-perishable, high-calorie foods that require minimal preparation, such as energy bars, dehydrated meals, and canned goods. Include a manual can opener if you carry canned food. It's also wise to have a small portable stove or a metal container for boiling water and cooking, along with a set of lightweight utensils.

Shelter is vital for protecting yourself from the elements. Exposure to extreme weather can lead to hypothermia or heatstroke, both of which are life-threatening. Your kit should contain a durable, all-weather emergency blanket or bivy sack. These items are compact, lightweight, and designed to reflect body heat, keeping you warm in cold conditions. A lightweight tarp and some paracord can be used to construct a makeshift shelter, providing additional protection from rain, wind, and sun.

A comprehensive first aid kit is indispensable. Injuries can occur at any time, and knowing how to treat wounds, fractures, burns, and other common injuries can prevent complications and save lives. Your first aid kit should include adhesive bandages, sterile gauze pads, adhesive tape, antiseptic wipes, a pair of tweezers, scissors, pain relievers, and any personal medications you require. Familiarize yourself with the contents of your first aid kit and understand how to use each item. Taking a first aid course will further enhance your ability to manage medical emergencies.

Navigation tools are crucial for finding your way to safety. A map of the area and a reliable compass should be standard items in your kit. While GPS devices and smartphones are useful, they rely on batteries and signals, which may not always be available. Learning to read a topographical map and use a compass ensures you can navigate even when technology fails. Including a whistle in your kit can help you signal for help, as its sound carries farther than a human voice.

Another essential item is a multi-tool or a sturdy knife. These versatile tools can assist with a variety of tasks, from preparing food to building shelter and making repairs. A high-quality multi-tool typically includes a knife blade, pliers, screwdrivers, and other useful implements. A fixed-blade knife is also valuable for more demanding tasks. Ensure your knife is kept sharp and practice using it safely.

Lighting is crucial for visibility and safety in the dark. Your kit should include a reliable flashlight with extra batteries or a hand-crank model that doesn't rely on batteries. Headlamps are particularly useful, as they allow you to keep your hands free while illuminating your surroundings. Consider including a pack of chemical light sticks as a backup; they provide a steady light source without the need for batteries.

Communication devices are vital for staying informed and reaching out for help. A battery-powered or hand-crank radio can keep you updated on weather conditions and emergency broadcasts. A fully charged cell phone and a portable charger or solar charger will help you maintain contact with loved ones and emergency services. In remote areas, a personal locator beacon (PLB) or satellite messenger can be a lifesaver, allowing you to send distress signals and your location to rescuers.

Clothing and personal items should be tailored to your environment and the season. Pack layers of clothing that can be added or removed as needed, including a waterproof jacket, sturdy footwear, and a hat. Extra socks and underwear are essential for maintaining hygiene and comfort. Include personal hygiene items such as a toothbrush, toothpaste, soap, and a small towel. Insect repellent and sunscreen are crucial for protecting your skin from bites and burns.

Cash and important documents should also be part of your kit. In the event of an emergency, ATMs and credit card systems may be down. Having a small amount of cash in various denominations can help you purchase supplies or services. Keep copies of important documents, such as identification, insurance policies, and emergency contact information, in a waterproof container or ziplock bag.

Lastly, consider the specific needs of any pets or young children in your family. Pack extra food, water, and supplies for them, including any medications and comfort items. Having appropriate gear for all members of your household ensures everyone is adequately prepared.

A well-organized and thoughtfully stocked survival kit can provide peace of mind and essential resources in an emergency. Regularly review and update your kit to ensure all items are in good condition and relevant to your current situation. By taking the time to prepare now, you'll be ready to face unexpected challenges with confidence and resilience.

Customizing Your Kit for Different Scenarios

Emergencies can arise in many forms, and no two situations are exactly alike. Whether you're facing a natural disaster, a prolonged power outage, or a sudden evacuation, having a customized kit tailored to specific scenarios is essential for effective preparedness. A one-size-fits-all approach to emergency kits can leave you unprepared for unique challenges. This chapter delves into the art of customizing your kit to suit various scenarios, ensuring you have the right tools and supplies for any situation.

When preparing for natural disasters, it's crucial to consider the specific threats prevalent in your region. For instance, residents in earthquake-prone areas should prioritize items that can protect them from falling debris and assist in navigating through rubble. Sturdy gloves, a hard hat, and a dust mask are indispensable in such scenarios. Including a crowbar or multi-tool capable of prying open jammed doors can be a lifesaver. Additionally, emergency whistles can help signal for rescue when trapped.

For those living in hurricane zones, the focus shifts to waterproofing and storm protection. Water-resistant containers and bags will keep your essentials dry. A battery-operated weather radio is vital for receiving updates when power lines are down. Since hurricanes often lead to extended periods without electricity, stock up on non-perishable food and a portable stove. An emergency generator can provide crucial power, but be sure to store enough fuel safely. Tarps and duct tape will help secure your home against wind and water damage.

Flooding presents another unique set of challenges. If you reside in a floodplain, your kit should include waterproof gear and tools for quick evacuation. Inflatable life vests and a small inflatable raft can be essential if escape routes are submerged. Keep important documents in a watertight container and have an emergency contact list written on waterproof paper. A portable water filter is crucial, as floodwaters can contaminate drinking supplies. Include heavy-duty trash bags for disposing of water-damaged items and debris.

Urban scenarios, such as city-wide power outages or civil unrest, require a different approach. In densely populated areas, mobility and stealth are key. A compact, easily transportable bag, often referred to as a "go-bag," should contain essentials for quick evacuation. Cash in small denominations is crucial, as ATMs and card readers may be inoperable. A tactical flashlight with a strobe function can serve as both a light source and a self-defense tool. Noise-canceling earplugs help maintain focus in chaotic environments. Also, consider a portable phone charger and a pre-paid cell phone to stay connected if networks are compromised.

In rural settings, where help may be farther away, self-sufficiency is paramount. Your kit should include items that enable you to live off the land if necessary. A comprehensive first aid kit with supplies for treating animal bites or stings is crucial. Tools for hunting, fishing, and foraging, such as a reliable knife, fishing line, and a field guide to edible plants, can extend your food supply. A durable compass and detailed topographic maps ensure you can navigate without relying on electronic devices. Given the isolation, a satellite phone or personal locator beacon provides a critical lifeline for contacting emergency services.

When traveling, whether for business or pleasure, your emergency kit must be adapted to fit your destination and mode of transport. For air travel, restrictions on liquids and sharp objects necessitate a pared-down version of your kit. Focus on items like a compact first aid kit, a power bank for electronic devices, and a universal travel adapter. If traveling internationally, include a copy of your passport, travel insurance details, and local emergency contact numbers. For road trips, ensure your vehicle is equipped with a robust emergency kit, including a spare tire, jack, and jumper cables. Pack extra water, snacks, and blankets in case you become stranded.

For those with specific medical needs, customizing your kit to include necessary medications and medical equipment is non-negotiable. Always have an ample supply of prescription medications, along with a copy of the prescription and a letter from your doctor detailing your medical needs. If you rely on medical devices that require power, such as insulin pumps or

CPAP machines, ensure you have portable power sources and backup batteries. Include a detailed medical history and emergency contact information for your healthcare providers.

Families with young children must consider additional supplies tailored to their needs. Diapers, formula, baby food, and comfort items like blankets or stuffed animals are essential. Activities to keep children occupied, such as coloring books and small toys, can help manage stress during emergencies. For households with pets, ensure you have pet food, water, and any medications they require. A pet carrier or leash will help manage your pets safely during evacuations.

Education and practice are crucial in ensuring your customized kit is effective. Regularly review and update your kit to account for changing needs and conditions. Conducting drills and practicing evacuation routes with your family will help everyone become familiar with the process and reduce panic during an actual emergency. Tailoring your kit to specific scenarios also involves staying informed about potential threats and having a clear understanding of the risks in your area.

Remember, the goal of customizing your kit is to enhance your resilience and readiness for a variety of situations. By carefully considering the unique challenges posed by different scenarios, you can ensure that your kit contains the most relevant and useful items. Preparedness is not a one-time task but an ongoing process that requires attention and adaptation. With a well-customized kit, you can face emergencies with confidence and the assurance that you have the tools needed to protect yourself and your loved ones. Given the dynamic nature of emergencies, flexibility and adaptability are key traits of an effective survival kit. As seasons change and new threats emerge, regularly reassess the contents of your kit to ensure they remain relevant and functional. This commitment to continuous improvement will enhance your preparedness and peace of mind.

Budget-Friendly Survival Kits

Crafting a survival kit on a budget is not only feasible but also essential for ensuring preparedness without financial strain. Many people believe that comprehensive survival kits require significant investment, but with strategic planning and resourcefulness, you can assemble an effective kit without breaking the bank. This chapter explores practical ways to build a budget-friendly survival kit, emphasizing cost-effective strategies, creative solutions, and prioritization of critical items.

The first step in creating a budget-friendly survival kit is to identify the essential items you will need. Focus on the core categories of water, food, shelter, first aid, tools, and communication. Begin by making a list of these necessities and then seek out affordable options within each category. For instance, bottled water is inexpensive and widely available. Stock up during sales or buy in bulk to save money. Additionally, consider water purification tablets or a small, portable water filter, which can treat large quantities of water over time and are cost-effective alternatives to constantly purchasing bottled water.

Food is another critical component where you can save money by purchasing wisely. Non-perishable items such as canned goods, rice, pasta, and beans are not only inexpensive but also have long shelf lives. Look for sales and discounts at grocery stores and consider buying store-brand products, which often cost less than name-brand items while offering similar quality. Another budget-friendly option is to buy in bulk from wholesale stores, which can significantly reduce the cost per unit. Don't forget to include a manual can opener in your kit, as it is a small but essential tool for accessing canned food.

Shelter and warmth are vital for survival, particularly in harsh conditions. Instead of investing in expensive tents or sleeping bags, consider more economical alternatives such as emergency blankets and plastic tarps. Emergency blankets, also known as space blankets, are extremely affordable and highly effective at retaining body heat. A plastic tarp, combined with some paracord, can serve as a makeshift shelter to protect you from the elements. Thrift stores and garage sales are excellent places to find additional budget-friendly items like blankets and sturdy clothing that can provide extra warmth.

A well-stocked first aid kit is crucial, but it doesn't have to be costly. Basic first aid supplies, such as adhesive bandages, antiseptic wipes, gauze pads, and pain relievers, are available at dollar stores and discount retailers. Many stores sell pre-assembled first aid kits at reasonable prices, which can be a good starting point. You can then customize and expand the kit with additional items based on your specific needs. Don't overlook the value of learning basic first aid skills, as knowledge is a powerful and free tool that enhances your ability to handle medical emergencies.

When it comes to tools and equipment, prioritize multifunctional items to get the most value for your money. A high-quality multi-tool can perform various tasks, reducing the need for multiple single-use tools. Look for sales, discounts, and second-hand options to find affordable tools. A sturdy knife, flashlight, and a basic set of hand tools are essential components that can be acquired without spending a fortune. Batteries for flashlights and other devices are often available in bulk at a lower cost, so stock up during sales to ensure you have an adequate supply.

Communication devices, such as a battery-powered or hand-crank radio, are essential for receiving emergency updates and staying informed. These radios are relatively inexpensive, and hand-crank models eliminate the need for batteries, providing a cost-effective solution. In addition, consider including a whistle in your kit, which is a very affordable tool for signaling for help.

Incorporate DIY solutions where possible to save money and personalize your kit. For example, you can create your own fire starters using household items like cotton balls coated in petroleum jelly, which are highly effective and inexpensive. Similarly, repurpose empty containers, such as plastic bottles and jars, for storing small items and organizing your kit. Sewing your own pouches and bags from durable fabric remnants can help keep items organized and accessible.

Another strategy for building a budget-friendly survival kit is to take advantage of community resources. Many communities offer free or low-cost emergency preparedness classes and workshops that provide valuable information and skills. Attending these events can also connect you with others who are interested in preparedness, allowing you to share resources and tips. Local government websites and libraries often provide free guides and checklists for emergency preparedness, which can help you prioritize items and plan effectively without incurring additional costs.

Building a network of friends and family who are also focused on emergency preparedness can be mutually beneficial. Pooling resources and sharing the cost of bulk purchases can reduce individual expenses while ensuring everyone is better prepared. For example, buying a case of batteries or a bulk pack of canned goods and splitting the cost among several people can be more economical than purchasing smaller quantities individually.

Regularly reassess and update your kit to ensure all items are in good condition and relevant to your needs. Rotate food and water supplies to maintain freshness and replace expired items. This ongoing maintenance can prevent the need for large, sudden expenditures by spreading costs over time and avoiding waste.

Remember that the effectiveness of your survival kit is not determined by how much you spend but by how well it meets your needs. By focusing on essential items, seeking out cost-effective solutions, and utilizing DIY and community resources, you can assemble a comprehensive and reliable survival kit on a budget. Preparedness is about planning, resourcefulness, and adaptability, and with these principles in mind, you can achieve a high level of readiness without financial strain.

Maintaining and Updating Your Kit

A survival kit is only as good as its contents, and those contents must be in good condition and up-to-date to be useful when needed. Regular maintenance and updates ensure that your kit remains effective and reliable over time. Neglecting this critical aspect can lead to expired food, non-functional equipment, and an overall lack of readiness. This chapter focuses on the practical steps you can take to maintain and update your survival kit, making sure it is always prepared for any emergency.

The first step is to establish a routine for checking your kit. A quarterly inspection is a good rule of thumb, but depending on your specific circumstances and the types of items in your kit, you might need to adjust this frequency. Set a reminder on your calendar to review your kit every three months. During these inspections, examine each item for signs of wear and tear, functionality, and expiration dates.

For perishable items like food and water, it is crucial to monitor expiration dates closely. Canned goods, while long-lasting, do not last forever. Check the labels and rotate these items regularly. When you notice that a product's expiration date is approaching, use it in your regular meal planning and replace it with a fresh item. This practice, known as FIFO (First In, First

Out), ensures that your emergency supplies are always within their usable lifespan.

Water storage is equally important. If you have bottled water in your kit, check the expiration date and replace it as necessary. For those using larger water containers, consider treating the water with purification tablets or rotating the water supply every six months. This helps prevent contamination and ensures that you have access to clean drinking water during an emergency.

Beyond food and water, batteries are another critical component that requires regular attention. Batteries have a limited shelf life and can leak or lose their charge over time. Check all battery-operated devices, such as flashlights and radios, and replace the batteries as needed. Consider investing in rechargeable batteries and a solar charger, which can be a more sustainable and cost-effective solution in the long run.

First aid supplies are essential for any survival kit and must be kept in optimal condition. Bandages, antiseptics, and medications all have expiration dates. Regularly review these items and replace anything that is expired or damaged. Additionally, consider any changes in your personal health needs. If you or a family member develop a new medical condition, update your first aid kit to include any necessary medications or supplies.

Tools and equipment should also be checked for functionality and condition. Inspect your multi-tools, knives, and other gear for rust, wear, and damage. Sharpen blades and oil moving parts to keep them in working order. If you discover that a tool is no longer functional, replace it promptly. It's also a good idea to practice using your tools periodically to ensure you are familiar with their operation and can use them effectively in an emergency.

Clothing and shelter items, such as blankets, tarps, and extra clothing, should be inspected for signs of wear and tear. Look for holes, fraying, or other damage that could compromise their effectiveness. Replace any items that are no longer in good condition. Additionally, consider the season and climate changes. In winter, you may need to add extra layers or thermal blankets, while in summer, lightweight, breathable fabrics might be more appropriate.

Communication devices, such as radios and cell phones, are vital for staying informed and connected during emergencies. Regularly test these devices to ensure they are working correctly. Verify that you have a reliable means of charging them, such as a battery pack or solar charger. Update any contact information stored on these devices and make sure you have a list of emergency contacts written down in case digital devices fail.

Documentation is another often overlooked aspect of maintaining your survival kit. Keep copies of important documents, such as identification, insurance papers, and medical records, in a waterproof container within your kit. Periodically review these documents to ensure they are current and complete. If you move or make significant life changes, update your documentation accordingly.

Finally, involve your family in the maintenance and updating process. Hold regular family meetings to review the contents of your survival kit and discuss any changes or updates. This not only ensures that everyone is aware of what is in the kit and how to use it, but it also helps to foster a sense of shared responsibility and preparedness. Encourage family members to suggest improvements and additions based on their own needs and experiences.

Maintaining and updating your survival kit is not a one-time task but an ongoing commitment. By establishing a routine, paying attention to details, and involving your family, you can ensure that your kit remains ready for any emergency. The peace of mind that comes from knowing you are prepared is invaluable, and the effort you put into regular maintenance will pay off when it matters most. Stay vigilant, stay prepared, and your survival kit will serve you well in times of need.

Portable vs. Stationary Kits

When preparing for emergencies, one of the key considerations is the type of survival kit you need: portable or stationary. Each serves a different purpose and has unique advantages and drawbacks. Understanding these differences is crucial in building a comprehensive preparedness plan that ensures you are ready for various scenarios, whether you need to evacuate quickly or shelter in place.

Portable kits, often referred to as "bug-out bags" (BOBs), are designed for mobility. These kits are compact, lightweight, and packed with essential items that you can carry with you if you need to leave your home in a hurry. The goal is to sustain you for at least 72 hours, covering the critical period after an emergency when help may not be immediately available. A well-prepared portable kit includes items such as water, non-perishable food, a first aid kit, a flashlight, batteries, a multi-tool, and important personal documents.

Water is one of the most critical components of a portable kit. A general guideline is to include at least one liter of water per person per day. However, carrying large amounts of water can be impractical due to weight constraints. Therefore, including water purification methods like tablets or a portable filter can be more efficient. Non-perishable food items should be high in calories and nutrients, such as energy bars, dried fruits, and nuts, which provide sustenance without taking up much space.

First aid supplies are indispensable in a portable kit. Basic items like adhesive bandages, antiseptic wipes, pain relievers, and any personal medications should be included. Additionally, a compact first aid manual can be incredibly useful in guiding you through medical emergencies. Tools like a multi-tool or a Swiss Army knife offer versatility without adding significant weight. They can assist with various tasks, from opening cans to cutting rope.

Clothing should be carefully selected to match the climate and season. Layering is key, as it allows you to adjust to changing weather conditions. Include a lightweight, waterproof jacket, a hat, gloves, and an extra pair of socks. Emergency blankets or space blankets are excellent for retaining body heat while being incredibly compact and lightweight.

Communication tools are vital in a portable kit. A battery-powered or hand-crank radio can keep you informed about emergency updates and weather conditions. Including a whistle and a small mirror can help signal for help if you find yourself in a situation where you need to attract attention. A fully charged power bank can keep your phone operational, ensuring you can stay connected with loved ones or emergency services.

On the other hand, stationary kits, sometimes called "stay-in-place" or "shelter-in-place" kits, are designed to support you at home or another fixed location for an extended period. These kits are larger and more comprehensive, as you do not need to worry about portability. They can include bulkier items that offer greater comfort and sustainability over time.

Water storage for a stationary kit should be more substantial. Aim for at least one gallon of water per person per day, with a supply lasting at least two weeks. Large water containers or barrels can be used, along with a water purification system to ensure a steady supply of clean water. Food supplies can include more variety and quantity, such as canned goods, dried beans, rice, pasta, and other shelf-stable items. Be sure to have a manual can opener and utensils for food preparation.

First aid supplies in a stationary kit should be comprehensive. Include a wider range of medications, bandages, antiseptics, and specialty items like splints or burn treatments. A more detailed first aid manual can provide in-depth guidance for various medical situations.

Tools and equipment for a stationary kit can be more extensive than those in a portable kit. Include items like a full-sized axe, a shovel, and a comprehensive tool kit. These can help with tasks like clearing debris, repairing shelter, or even building new structures if necessary. Power tools with a sufficient supply of batteries or a generator can be incredibly useful in maintaining your home during prolonged emergencies.

Comfort items can also play a significant role in a stationary kit. Consider including extra blankets, pillows, and even entertainment options like books or board games to help pass the time and maintain morale. Personal hygiene items, such as soap, toothbrushes, toothpaste, and sanitary products, should be stocked in sufficient quantities to last for several weeks.

Communication tools in a stationary kit can include more robust options, such as a ham radio, which can provide long-range communication capabilities. A generator or solar power system can ensure that you have a reliable source of electricity to keep your devices charged and operational.

Both portable and stationary kits have their place in a well-rounded preparedness strategy. The choice between them depends on the specific threats you are preparing for and your personal circumstances. Ideally, you should have both types of kits ready to cover a wide range of scenarios.

For instance, if you live in an area prone to natural disasters like hurricanes or wildfires, having a portable kit ready to go can be crucial for quick evacuations. Meanwhile, a stationary kit can help you weather the aftermath when returning home might not be immediately possible. Urban dwellers might prioritize portable kits due to the higher likelihood of needing to move quickly, whereas those in rural areas might focus more on stationary kits due to the potential for isolation during emergencies.

Regularly reviewing and updating both types of kits is essential. Check expiration dates on food, water, and medications, and replace them as needed. Update personal documents and contact information, and ensure all equipment is in working order. Practicing with your portable kit can help you identify any missing items or inefficiencies, while maintaining your stationary kit can ensure you are comfortable and safe during extended periods of sheltering in place.

In conclusion, both portable and stationary kits are vital components of emergency preparedness. Each serves distinct purposes and offers unique benefits. By understanding the differences and planning accordingly, you can ensure that you are equipped to handle a variety of emergency situations, whether you need to evacuate quickly or remain at home for an extended period. Stay prepared, stay vigilant, and your readiness will provide peace of mind and security in uncertain times.

Chapter 3: Water Procurement and Purification

Finding Water Sources

Locating water sources in an emergency situation can be a matter of life or death. Whether you're in an urban environment during a municipal water outage or stranded in the wilderness, understanding how to find and purify water is crucial. This chapter delves into practical strategies and actionable tips to help you secure water when conventional supplies are unavailable.

Water is essential for survival, and the human body can only last about three days without it. The first step in finding water is to understand where to look. In urban areas, you might initially check your home for hidden water reserves. Start with your water heater, which can hold 30-50 gallons of potable water. Ensure the heater is turned off and let the water cool before accessing it. To extract the water, connect a hose to the drain valve at the bottom of the tank. Remember to have a container ready to catch the liquid.

Another urban source is the water trapped in your pipes. If the water system is contaminated or shut off, you can still access this water by opening the highest faucet in your home to let air into the pipes, then collecting water from the lowest faucet. Toilets, too, hold usable water in their tanks (not bowls), provided no chemical cleaners have been added. Cover the tank with a clean cloth to filter out any debris before drinking.

In rural or wilderness settings, natural sources like rivers, streams, and lakes are your best bet. Flowing water is generally safer than stagnant water, as it is less likely to harbor harmful bacteria. When searching for rivers or streams, follow the terrain downhill, as water naturally flows to lower elevations. Vegetation can also be a clue; lush, green areas often indicate nearby water sources.

Morning dew can be a lifesaver when other sources are not available. Use absorbent cloths or even your clothing to collect dew from grass and leaves in the early morning hours. Wring out the water into a container. While this method won't provide large quantities of water, it can help in a pinch.

Rainwater is another viable option. Use tarps, plastic sheets, or even large leaves to funnel rain into containers. Position your collection system to maximize the surface area exposed to rainfall. Store the collected water in clean, covered containers to avoid contamination.

If natural sources are scarce, look for signs of animal activity. Birds, especially those that eat grains, often fly towards water sources at dawn and dusk. Following their flight paths can lead you to water. Additionally, many animals create trails leading to water sources. Deer paths, for example, are often reliable indicators of nearby streams or ponds.

In arid environments, water can sometimes be found by digging in dry riverbeds. Look for areas where the sand or soil is slightly damp. Dig a hole about a foot deep and wait for water to seep in. This water will need to be filtered and purified before drinking.

In coastal areas, desalination becomes a necessary skill. Constructing a solar still can convert saltwater into freshwater. Dig a hole in the sand above the high tide line, place a container in the center, and cover the hole with plastic sheeting. Weigh down the edges of the sheet with rocks and place a small stone in the center so that it dips towards the container. As the sun heats the sand, water will evaporate, condense on the plastic, and drip into the container.

Regardless of the source, all water collected must be purified before consumption to avoid waterborne illnesses. Boiling is the most reliable method, killing bacteria, viruses, and parasites. Bring the water to a rolling boil for at least one minute (or three minutes at altitudes above 6,500 feet).

If boiling is not an option, chemical purification can be effective. Household bleach (unscented) can be used; add eight drops per gallon of water, stir, and let it sit for 30 minutes. Water purification tablets, available at most outdoor stores, are another convenient option. Follow the instructions on the package for proper usage.

Filtration devices are also invaluable, particularly portable water filters designed for backpacking. These devices can remove bacteria and protozoa, though not all are effective against viruses. A combination of filtration and chemical treatment provides the best protection against all contaminants.

Solar disinfection (SODIS) is an alternative method, particularly useful in sunny climates. Fill clear plastic bottles with water and leave them in direct sunlight for six hours (or two days if the weather is cloudy). UV rays from the sun will kill most pathogens, making the water safe to drink.

Improvised filters can be made using materials like sand, charcoal, and gravel. Layer these materials in a container with holes at the bottom, and pour water through. This method helps remove particulates but should be followed by boiling or chemical treatment to ensure safety.

In survival situations, it's crucial to conserve water. Avoid strenuous activities during the heat of the day to reduce sweating, and stay in shaded areas whenever possible. Drink water regularly, even if you don't feel thirsty, to maintain hydration and avoid heat-related illnesses.

Understanding how to find and purify water is a fundamental survival skill. By knowing where to look and how to treat water from various sources, you can significantly increase your chances of staying hydrated and healthy in any emergency. Whether navigating an urban crisis or surviving in the wilderness, these techniques will help ensure you have access to this most vital resource.

Purification Methods

In any survival situation, ensuring access to clean, safe drinking water is paramount. Purification methods are essential for removing harmful pathogens, chemicals, and particulates from water, making it suitable for consumption. Understanding the various techniques available and knowing how to apply them effectively can mean the difference between health and illness, or even life and death.

Boiling is one of the simplest and most effective methods to purify water. By bringing water to a rolling boil for at least one minute, you can kill most bacteria, viruses, and parasites. At altitudes above 6,500 feet, it is advisable to boil water for three minutes due to the lower boiling point of water at higher elevations. Boiling does not remove chemical contaminants or heavy metals, but it ensures that biological pathogens are neutralized.

Chemical disinfection is another widely used method. Household bleach, containing 5-6% sodium hypochlorite, can be used to disinfect water. The general guideline is to add eight drops of bleach per gallon of water, stir, and let it sit for 30 minutes. The water should have a slight chlorine odor; if not, repeat the process. Be cautious with bleach, as using too much can be harmful. Water purification tablets, which often contain chlorine dioxide or iodine, are another convenient option. These tablets are lightweight, easy to carry, and effective against a broad range of pathogens. Follow the manufacturer's instructions carefully to ensure proper usage.

Filtration devices are incredibly useful, especially in the field. Portable water filters are designed to remove bacteria and protozoa, and some advanced models can also filter out viruses. These filters typically use a combination of activated carbon and ceramic or hollow fiber membranes. Activated carbon is particularly effective at removing chemical contaminants and improving taste and odor. When using a portable filter, ensure that the filter is properly maintained and regularly replaced to maintain its efficacy.

For those without access to commercial filters, constructing a homemade filter can be a viable option. Using materials such as sand, gravel, and activated charcoal, you can create a layered filtration system within a container. First, place a layer of gravel at the bottom, followed by sand, and then a layer of activated charcoal. Pouring water through this filter helps remove larger particulates and some chemical impurities. However, this method should be followed by boiling or chemical disinfection to ensure the water is biologically safe.

Solar disinfection, or SODIS, is a method that uses the sun's ultraviolet (UV) rays to purify water. Fill clear plastic bottles with water and leave them in direct sunlight for at least six hours. UV-A rays from the sun kill or inactivate harmful microorganisms, making the water safe to drink. This method is particularly useful in areas with abundant sunlight and limited resources. It is important to use clear, uncolored plastic bottles and to ensure that the bottles are not scratched or damaged, as this can reduce the effectiveness of the process.

Distillation is a more complex but highly effective purification method that removes a wide range of contaminants, including heavy metals, salts, and most pathogens. The process involves heating water to create steam, which is then collected and condensed back into liquid form, leaving impurities behind. A solar still is a practical application of this method in survival situations. Dig a hole in the ground, place a container in the center, and cover the hole with plastic sheeting, securing the edges with rocks. Place a small stone in the center of the plastic to create a low point directly above the container. As the sun heats the ground, water will evaporate, condense on the plastic, and drip into the container.

UV light purifiers are increasingly popular, particularly for travelers. These devices use ultraviolet light to kill bacteria, viruses, and protozoa. A common example is a UV pen, which can be submerged in a container of water and activated to purify the contents within minutes. This method is quick and effective, but it relies on battery power and does not remove particulates or chemical contaminants.

Charcoal filtering, while often used in combination with other methods, can also stand alone as a purification technique. Activated charcoal has a large surface area that adsorbs impurities, improving the taste and odor of water. A simple charcoal filter can be made by filling a container with activated charcoal and passing water through it. This method is particularly effective at removing organic compounds and chlorine, but it should be followed by additional purification steps to ensure biological safety.

In some situations, emergency purification methods may be necessary. Improvised filters using cloth or coffee filters can remove larger particulates from water. While these methods do not guarantee biological safety, they can be a first step before applying other purification techniques. Additionally, natural coagulants like crushed Moringa seeds or alum can be used to clarify water by binding with particles and causing them to settle out of suspension. This process should be followed by boiling or chemical disinfection.

Maintaining hygiene and proper handling of purified water is crucial to prevent recontamination. Store purified water in clean, covered containers and avoid touching the inside of the container or the water with unclean hands or utensils. Regularly clean and sterilize storage containers to ensure they remain free of contaminants.

Understanding the strengths and limitations of each purification method allows you to choose the most appropriate technique for your situation. Combining methods can provide an added layer of safety. For example, filtering water before boiling or using chemical disinfection can ensure that both particulates and pathogens are effectively removed.

In any survival scenario, access to safe drinking water is a top priority. By mastering various purification methods, you can ensure that you and your loved ones have a reliable supply of clean water, regardless of the circumstances. This knowledge not only enhances your preparedness but also provides peace of mind in knowing that you can handle one of the most critical aspects of survival.

Long-Term Water Storage

Long-term water storage is a critical aspect of preparedness, ensuring that you and your family have access to safe drinking water during extended emergencies. Whether facing natural disasters, infrastructure failures, or other crises, having a sufficient supply of stored water can provide peace of mind and security. To effectively store water long-term, it's essential to understand the various methods, containers, and treatment options available.

The first step in long-term water storage is determining how much water you need. The general recommendation is to store at least one gallon of water per person per day for drinking and sanitation. For a family of four, a two-week supply would amount to 56 gallons. This calculation can help you plan the amount of water to store based on your household size and expected duration of the emergency.

Selecting appropriate containers is crucial for maintaining the quality of stored water. Food-grade plastic containers, such as those made from high-density polyethylene (HDPE), are ideal for long-term storage. These containers are durable, non-reactive, and designed to prevent contamination. Avoid using containers that previously held chemicals or non-food substances, as they can leach harmful contaminants into the water.

Large water storage barrels, typically holding 55 gallons, are a popular choice for long-term storage. These barrels are usually blue to indicate they are food-grade and to reduce algae growth by blocking sunlight. When using large barrels, ensure they are placed on a sturdy, level surface and are easily accessible in case of an emergency. Smaller containers, like 5-gallon jugs or water bricks, offer versatility and portability. These can be stacked and stored in various locations around your home, ensuring you have access to water in different areas.

Before filling your containers, it's essential to clean and sanitize them properly. Wash the containers with dish soap and water, then rinse thoroughly. Sanitize by adding a solution of one teaspoon of unscented household bleach per quart of water, swishing it around to coat all surfaces, and letting it sit for at least 30 seconds. Rinse the container with clean water before filling it with potable water.

Filling your containers with safe, treated water is crucial. If you're using tap water from a municipal supply, it's generally safe to assume it's already treated and potable. However, if you're using well water or another source, it's advisable to treat it before storage. Boiling the water for one minute (or three minutes at higher elevations) or using water purification tablets can ensure it's safe to store.

Once your containers are filled, proper storage conditions are key to maintaining water quality. Store water in a cool, dark place, away from direct sunlight and temperature extremes. Heat can accelerate the deterioration of plastic containers, and sunlight can promote algae growth. Ideal storage locations include basements, closets, or under beds. Rotate your water supply every six months to ensure freshness. Mark the containers with the date they were filled, and use the oldest water first. While water itself doesn't go bad, the containers can degrade over time, leading to possible contamination.

For extended emergencies, having a system for collecting and storing additional water can be beneficial. Rainwater harvesting systems, which collect and store rainwater from rooftops, can provide a supplemental water source. Ensure that the collection system is equipped with a first flush diverter to remove debris and contaminants from the initial flow of water. Stored rainwater should be treated before use to ensure it's safe for drinking.

In addition to storing water for drinking, consider your needs for hygiene and sanitation. Storing extra water for handwashing, cleaning, and flushing toilets is essential. Non-potable water sources, such as rainwater or water from a pond or stream, can be used for these purposes if treated appropriately.

Emergency water storage doesn't end with just having the water; having the right tools and knowledge to access and use it during a crisis is equally important. A siphon pump can be useful for accessing water from large barrels without having to tip them over. Keeping a supply of water purification tablets, filters, and a portable stove for boiling water can provide additional layers of safety and flexibility.

It's also important to consider the psychological and practical aspects of long-term water storage. Regularly involve your family in checking and rotating the water supply. This practice not only ensures that everyone knows where and how to access the water but also reinforces the importance of preparedness. Having a well-organized and easily accessible water storage system can reduce stress and anxiety during an emergency, allowing you to focus on other critical aspects of survival.

Incorporating long-term water storage into your overall emergency preparedness plan is a proactive step towards ensuring your family's safety and well-being. By understanding the best practices for storing, treating, and accessing water, you can build a reliable and sustainable water supply that will serve you well in times of need. Remember, water is an essential resource, and taking the time to store it properly can make all the difference in an emergency.

Building a Rainwater Collection System

Building a rainwater collection system is an essential skill for anyone looking to become more self-sufficient and sustainable. This method of water harvesting can provide a reliable source of water for various uses, especially in times of drought or water restrictions. Setting up an effective system requires planning, understanding the components, and ensuring proper maintenance. This chapter will guide you through the steps necessary to build and maintain a rainwater collection system.

The first step in building a rainwater collection system is selecting the appropriate site. Ideally, you want a site that has a large roof area to maximize water capture. The roof material should be non-toxic and safe for collecting water. Metal roofs are ideal because they are smooth and facilitate easy runoff. Avoid roofs with asbestos, lead paint, or treated wood shingles, as these can contaminate the water. Additionally, the site should be close to where you will use the water to minimize the need for extensive piping.

Once you have chosen the site, the next step is to install gutters and downspouts. Gutters should be installed along the edges of the roof to catch the rainwater. These gutters should slope slightly towards the downspouts to ensure water flows efficiently. Downspouts direct the water from the gutters to your storage tanks. It's crucial to install screens or guards on the gutters to keep out leaves, twigs, and other debris that could clog the system.

Before the water reaches the storage tanks, it's important to install a first flush diverter. This device diverts the initial flow of rainwater away from the storage tanks to remove roof debris and contaminants that accumulate during dry periods. The first flush diverter typically consists of a pipe that captures the first few gallons of runoff, which is then discarded or used for non-potable purposes. This step is vital for ensuring the quality of the water stored in your tanks.

Selecting the right storage tanks is another critical component. Tanks come in various sizes and materials, including plastic, fiberglass, and metal. Plastic tanks are popular due to their durability, affordability, and resistance to corrosion. When choosing a tank, consider the amount of rainfall in your area and the size of your roof to determine the capacity you need. For example, a 1,000-square-foot roof can collect approximately 600 gallons of water per inch of rainfall. Ensure the tank is food-grade if you plan to use the water for drinking or cooking.

Position the tanks on a solid, level base. Concrete pads or compacted gravel bases are ideal to support the weight of a full tank. The tanks should be placed in a shaded area to prevent algae growth and reduce evaporation. Connecting multiple tanks in series can increase your storage capacity and provide redundancy in case one tank fails.

Plumbing the system is the next step. Use PVC pipes to connect the downspouts to the storage tanks. Install a filter or fine mesh screen at the tank inlets to prevent insects and small debris from entering. It's also a good idea to include a shut-off valve between the downspouts and the tanks to control the flow of water. Inside the tanks, install an overflow pipe to direct excess water away from the foundation of your home, preventing potential damage.

To access the stored water, install a spigot or hose connection at the bottom of the tank. This allows you to easily draw water for gardening, washing, or other uses. If you plan to use the water for drinking, consider installing a water pump and filtration system. Filters should be capable of removing bacteria, viruses, and other contaminants to ensure the water is safe for consumption.

Maintaining your rainwater collection system is crucial for its long-term effectiveness. Regularly inspect and clean the gutters, downspouts, and first flush diverter to remove any debris. Check the tanks for leaks and ensure the screens and filters are clean and functioning properly. During dry periods, monitor the water levels and use the stored water judiciously to avoid running out.

In addition to maintenance, it's important to be aware of any local regulations or codes regarding rainwater harvesting. Some areas have restrictions on the amount of water that can be collected or require permits for large storage systems. Complying with these regulations ensures your system is legal and avoids potential fines or penalties.

Building a rainwater collection system can provide numerous benefits, both environmental and economic. By harvesting rainwater, you reduce your reliance on municipal water supplies and conserve this precious resource. Rainwater is naturally soft and free of many chemicals found in tap water, making it ideal for watering plants and gardens. Additionally, using rainwater can lower your water bills and provide a backup supply during emergencies.

One anecdote that illustrates the value of a rainwater collection system comes from a family living in a drought-prone region. After enduring several dry seasons with water restrictions, they decided to invest in a comprehensive rainwater harvesting system. By collecting and storing rainwater from their roof, they were able to maintain a lush vegetable garden and keep their livestock hydrated, even during the driest months. The system not only provided a reliable water source but also gave them a sense of security and independence.

Another story involves a community that came together to install a large rainwater collection system at their local school. With the system in place, the school was able to use the collected rainwater for irrigation, reducing their dependence on the municipal water supply. The project also served as an educational tool, teaching students about water conservation and sustainable practices.

In conclusion, building a rainwater collection system is a practical and rewarding endeavor. It requires careful planning, the right materials, and regular maintenance, but the benefits far outweigh the efforts. By capturing and storing rainwater, you can ensure a reliable water supply, reduce your environmental impact, and gain greater self-sufficiency. Whether for personal use or as part of a community project, rainwater harvesting is a valuable skill that contributes to a sustainable and resilient future.

DIY Water Filters

Creating a DIY water filter can be a lifesaving skill, especially in situations where access to clean drinking water is compromised. Whether you're preparing for an emergency, camping in the wilderness, or looking to purify your water supply at home, understanding how to build an effective water filter from readily available materials is invaluable. This chapter delves into the practical steps and considerations for constructing your own water filters, ensuring that you have safe water no matter the circumstance.

The first principle of any water filter is to remove contaminants, which can range from sediment and organic matter to bacteria and viruses. To achieve this, a typical DIY water filter will use multiple layers of different materials, each serving a specific purpose in the filtration process.

Start with the container that will hold your filter materials. A two-liter plastic bottle is commonly used due to its availability and ease of handling, but any food-grade container can work. Cut off the bottom of the bottle, leaving the cap on. This will be where you pour in the contaminated water. The cap should have a small hole to allow water to drip through slowly, ensuring maximum contact with the filter materials.

The first layer in your filter should be a coffee filter or a piece of cloth. This acts as a preliminary screen, catching larger debris and preventing the finer filter materials from falling out. Secure this layer over the opening where the cap is, using a rubber band or string if necessary.

Next, add a layer of activated charcoal. Activated charcoal is highly porous and effective at removing many organic contaminants, odors, and some chemicals. You can purchase activated charcoal from pet stores (often marketed for aquarium filters) or make it by heating wood in the absence of air. Ensure the charcoal is crushed into small granules to maximize its surface area.

Above the charcoal, place a layer of fine sand. The sand helps remove smaller particulates and works in conjunction with the charcoal to filter out impurities. Ensure the sand is clean and free of contaminants by rinsing it thoroughly before use. Fine sand is preferable because it provides a more effective barrier against tiny particles.

The next layer should be coarser sand or small pebbles. This layer helps to filter out larger particles before they reach the finer sand and charcoal layers. It also helps to distribute the water evenly across the filter, ensuring that it flows through all the layers effectively.

The final layer is gravel. This serves to remove the largest debris and helps to prevent the finer sand and charcoal from being disturbed when you pour water into the filter. Like the sand, ensure the gravel is clean by washing it thoroughly.

With all the layers in place, your DIY water filter is ready to use. To operate the filter, pour water into the open bottom of the bottle (the top, if the bottle is upside down). The water will pass through each layer, with the different materials removing various contaminants. Collect the filtered water from the cap end of the bottle.

While this filter can significantly improve the clarity and quality of water, it is essential to understand that it may not remove all pathogens. For complete safety, filtered water should be boiled for at least one minute (or three minutes at higher altitudes) to kill any remaining bacteria, viruses, or parasites. Alternatively, you can use water purification tablets or UV purification devices as an additional treatment step.

In addition to the basic filter described above, there are several enhancements and variations you can consider. For instance, adding a layer of cotton balls or cheesecloth between the gravel and coarse sand can help further refine the filtration process. You can also experiment with different container sizes and shapes, depending on your specific needs and the materials available.

For those who anticipate long-term use or want a more permanent solution, consider constructing a larger, more robust filter system. This could involve using a series of buckets with holes drilled in the bottoms, stacked in sequence with the same layered materials. Such a system can handle larger volumes of water and may be suitable for household use or group settings.

Maintenance of your DIY water filter is crucial to ensure its continued effectiveness. Over time, the filter materials can become clogged with trapped contaminants, reducing the flow rate and filtration quality. Regularly inspect the layers and replace the materials as needed. Activated charcoal loses its effectiveness after a while and should be replaced periodically. The frequency of maintenance will depend on the frequency of use and the quality of the water being filtered.

For those interested in understanding the science behind water filtration, it's helpful to know how each layer works. The gravel and coarse sand layers physically block larger particles, while the fine sand removes smaller particles through physical straining. Activated charcoal adsorbs organic compounds, chlorine, and some heavy metals, effectively trapping these contaminants within its porous structure. This multilayer approach ensures a comprehensive filtration process, enhancing the overall safety and palatability of the water.

One real-world example of the importance of DIY water filters comes from communities affected by natural disasters. In the aftermath of hurricanes, earthquakes, or floods, access to clean water can become severely restricted. DIY water filters, constructed from available materials, have provided vital relief in these emergencies, allowing affected individuals to obtain safe drinking water while awaiting more substantial aid.

Another scenario where DIY water filters prove invaluable is in remote or developing regions where access to commercial water filtration systems is limited. By teaching communities to build their own filters, we empower them to take control of their water quality, improving health outcomes and reducing the incidence of waterborne diseases.

In conclusion, learning to build a DIY water filter is a practical and empowering skill. It provides a reliable method for improving water quality in various situations, from emergency preparedness to everyday use in areas with questionable water supplies. By understanding the principles of filtration and the specific roles of different materials, you can create an effective system tailored to your needs. Remember to always follow up filtration with additional purification methods like boiling or chemical treatment to ensure the water is safe to drink. With this knowledge, you can confidently face water challenges, knowing you have the tools to provide clean, safe water for yourself and your loved ones.

Chapter 4: Food Acquisition and Preservation

Foraging for Edible Plants

Foraging for edible plants is a skill that taps into the abundance of nature and connects us with ancestral practices that sustained humans for millennia. While modern life often distances us from this knowledge, understanding how to identify, harvest, and use wild plants can enhance self-sufficiency and provide nutritious, free food sources. This chapter will guide you through the basics of foraging, offering practical advice on how to safely and effectively gather edible plants.

Before setting out on your foraging adventure, it is crucial to familiarize yourself with the local flora. Investing in a good field guide specific to your region is invaluable. These guides typically provide detailed descriptions, photographs, and information on the habitat and seasonality of plants. Alternatively, attending a foraging workshop or joining a local foraging group can offer hands-on learning experiences and mentorship from experienced foragers.

The cardinal rule of foraging is to positively identify any plant before consuming it. Many edible plants have toxic look-alikes, so careful observation and comparison with reliable sources are essential. Key identification features include leaf shape, flower structure, plant size, and growth habit. For example, wild garlic (Allium ursinum) can be identified by its broad, lance-shaped leaves and distinctive garlic smell, whereas its toxic look-alike, lily of the valley (Convallaria majalis), lacks this scent and has bell-shaped flowers.

Once you have identified a plant, consider its environment. Avoid foraging near roadsides, industrial areas, or places where pesticides and herbicides are likely used. These areas can expose plants to pollutants and chemicals that are harmful if ingested. Instead, seek out wild areas, forests, and meadows where plants are more likely to be free from contaminants.

When harvesting plants, practice sustainable foraging to ensure that the plant populations remain healthy and vibrant. This means taking only what you need and leaving enough for the plant to continue growing and reproducing. For instance, if you are gathering wild berries, pick from several plants rather than stripping one bush bare. This approach helps maintain the ecosystem and ensures future foragers will also find an abundance of food.

Common edible plants that are relatively easy to identify and widely available include dandelions (Taraxacumofficinale), nettles (Urticadioica), and chickweed (Stellaria media). Dandelions are particularly versatile, with every part of the plant being edible. The young leaves can be used in salads, the flowers can be made into wine or fritters, and the roots can be roasted as a coffee substitute. Nettles, despite their sting, are highly nutritious and can be cooked to neutralize their stinging hairs, making them suitable for soups, teas, and pestos. Chickweed, with its mild flavor, is excellent in salads or as a cooked green.

Understanding the nutritional benefits of wild plants can also enhance your foraging experience. Many wild edibles are packed with vitamins, minerals, and antioxidants. For example, stinging nettles are rich in iron, calcium, and vitamin C, making them a valuable addition to your diet. Similarly, wild berries like blackberries and blueberries are high in fiber and vitamin K, supporting overall health.

Safety should always be your top priority when foraging. In addition to proper plant identification, be aware of any personal allergies or sensitivities. Some individuals may react to certain plants even if they are generally considered safe to eat. Start with small amounts if you are trying a new plant for the first time and monitor for any adverse reactions.

Foraging also requires an understanding of the laws and regulations in your area. In some places, foraging is restricted or regulated to protect endangered species and maintain natural habitats. Always check local guidelines and obtain necessary permissions before foraging on public or private land. Respecting these rules helps preserve the environment and ensures that foraging remains a sustainable practice.

Beyond the practical aspects, foraging offers a unique way to connect with nature and appreciate the changing seasons. Spring brings tender shoots and blossoms, summer provides a bounty of fruits and greens, fall offers nuts and roots, and winter reveals hardy plants and fungi. Each season presents different opportunities and challenges, encouraging a deeper understanding of the natural world.

One story that illustrates the joy and utility of foraging comes from a family who began exploring their local woods during weekend hikes. They started by identifying common plants like wild garlic and elderflowers, gradually expanding their knowledge and skills. Over time, they were able to supplement their meals with foraged foods, from wild garlic pesto in the spring to elderflower cordial in the summer and blackberry jams in the fall. This practice not only enriched their diet but also fostered a sense of adventure and connection to their environment.

Another example involves a community group that organized foraging walks to educate members about local edible plants. These walks became a popular activity, bringing people together to share knowledge and experiences. The group even compiled a foraging calendar, highlighting which plants were available each month and how to use them. This initiative not only promoted sustainable living but also strengthened community bonds.

Foraging also has a role in emergency preparedness. In situations where food supplies are disrupted, the ability to identify and harvest wild edibles can be a critical survival skill. Knowing what plants are available in different seasons and how to prepare them can provide a valuable food source during crises. Practicing foraging regularly ensures that this knowledge is second nature when it is most needed.

In conclusion, foraging for edible plants is a rewarding practice that combines practical skills with a deeper connection to nature. By learning to identify, harvest, and use wild plants, you can enhance your self-sufficiency, improve your diet, and enjoy the richness of the natural world. Remember to prioritize safety, respect the environment, and share your knowledge with others. Whether you are a beginner or an experienced forager, there is always something new to discover and appreciate in the wild.

Hunting and Trapping

Hunting and trapping have long been essential skills for human survival, providing not only food but also materials for clothing, tools, and shelter. In modern times, these practices remain valuable for those seeking self-sufficiency, a deeper connection to nature, or simply an adventurous way to procure food. This chapter delves into the fundamentals of hunting and trapping, offering practical advice and insights for beginners while emphasizing ethical and sustainable practices.

Before embarking on any hunting or trapping expedition, it is crucial to understand the regulations and laws governing these activities in your area. Wildlife management agencies set rules to ensure sustainable populations and ethical treatment of animals. These regulations often include specific hunting seasons, bag limits, and licensing requirements. Familiarize yourself with these laws to avoid legal issues and contribute to conservation efforts.

Safety is paramount when handling firearms or traps. Proper training in firearm safety is essential, including how to handle, load, unload, and store weapons. Many regions offer hunter safety courses that provide comprehensive training and certification. When using traps, understand the mechanics and proper placement to avoid accidents. Always inform someone of your plans and expected return time before heading into the wilderness.

Successful hunting and trapping require a deep understanding of the behavior and habitats of your target species. Spend time researching and observing animals in their natural environments. Learn to identify tracks, scat, and other signs that indicate the presence of wildlife. Understanding the habits and routines of animals, such as feeding times and preferred shelter, increases your chances of a successful hunt or trap.

Selecting the appropriate equipment is crucial. For hunting, this includes choosing the right firearm or bow, ammunition, and accessories like scopes and sights. Consider the type of game you are pursuing; small game like rabbits and squirrels require different gear than larger animals like deer or elk. For trapping, a variety of traps are available, each designed for specific animals. Common traps include snares, leg-hold traps, and cage traps. Ensure you understand how to set and check them correctly.

Stealth and patience are essential traits for hunters. Animals have keen senses and can detect human presence through scent, sound, or movement. Wear camouflage appropriate for the environment and use scent-masking techniques. Move slowly and quietly, taking advantage of natural cover. Patience pays off; sometimes, remaining still for extended periods is necessary to avoid detection and wait for the right moment to strike.

Ethical hunting and trapping involve respect for the animals and the environment. Aim for clean, quick kills to minimize suffering. Practice shooting regularly to maintain accuracy and proficiency. When trapping, check traps frequently to ensure captured animals are not left to suffer. Use all parts of the animal whenever possible, honoring the life that has been taken by minimizing waste.

Field dressing and processing game are essential skills. Once an animal is harvested, it must be properly cleaned and prepared to prevent spoilage and make the meat safe for consumption. Field dressing involves removing the internal organs as soon as possible to cool the carcass. Learn the techniques for skinning, quartering, and butchering different types of game. Proper storage, such as refrigeration or freezing, is necessary to preserve meat until it can be consumed or processed further.

Hunting and trapping also offer valuable lessons in self-reliance and resourcefulness. For example, a seasoned hunter once shared a story of tracking a deer through dense forest for hours. The experience required not only physical stamina but also problem-solving skills and adaptability. When the deer finally presented a clear shot, the hunter's preparation and patience were rewarded. This kind of experience teaches resilience and the importance of preparation, traits that are valuable in many aspects of life.

Similarly, a trapper recounted the satisfaction of setting and checking a series of snares along a well-used animal trail. The ability to read the landscape, understand animal behavior, and strategically place traps led to a successful catch. This process highlighted the importance of knowledge and skill in achieving goals, reinforcing the connection between effort and reward.

Hunting and trapping can also foster a deeper appreciation for nature and the interconnectedness of ecosystems. Observing wildlife in their natural habitats and understanding their roles within the environment cultivates respect and a sense of stewardship. Many hunters and trappers become advocates for conservation, recognizing the need to protect habitats and ensure sustainable wildlife populations.

In addition to providing food, hunting and trapping can yield other valuable resources. Animal hides can be tanned and used for clothing, footwear, and gear. Bones and antlers can be fashioned into tools, utensils, and ornaments. Learning to utilize every part of the animal reduces waste and maximizes the benefits of your efforts.

For those new to hunting and trapping, seeking mentorship from experienced practitioners can be incredibly beneficial.

Joining a local hunting club or association provides opportunities to learn from seasoned hunters and trappers. These groups often organize training sessions, hunting trips, and social events that enhance skills and build camaraderie. Sharing experiences and knowledge within a community fosters growth and confidence.

Technology can also aid in hunting and trapping endeavors. Modern innovations such as trail cameras, GPS devices, and weather apps provide valuable information and enhance safety. Trail cameras placed along game trails or near food sources can reveal patterns in animal movement, helping you plan your hunts more effectively. GPS devices ensure you can navigate unfamiliar terrain and find your way back to camp. Weather apps provide up-to-date information on conditions that can influence animal behavior and hunting success.

While technology offers advantages, it is important to balance its use with traditional skills and knowledge. Relying too heavily on gadgets can detract from the immersive, skill-based experience that hunting and trapping provide. Strive to develop a comprehensive skill set that combines modern tools with fundamental techniques.

Finally, hunting and trapping require a significant time investment, but the rewards extend beyond the immediate harvest. The skills, knowledge, and experiences gained through these activities contribute to a sense of self-reliance and a deeper connection to the natural world. Whether you are preparing for a self-sufficient lifestyle, seeking adventure, or simply enjoying the outdoors, hunting and trapping offer a fulfilling and enriching pursuit.

In conclusion, hunting and trapping are multifaceted practices that combine skill, knowledge, and respect for nature. By understanding regulations, prioritizing safety, and honing your abilities, you can successfully harvest wild game and contribute to sustainable wildlife management. These activities not only provide food and resources but also foster a deeper appreciation for the natural world and the interconnectedness of ecosystems. Through patience, preparation, and ethical practices, hunting and trapping can become a rewarding and integral part of your self-sufficient lifestyle.

Fishing Techniques

Fishing is one of humanity's oldest practices, providing sustenance and fostering a deep connection with the natural world. For those seeking to enhance their self-sufficiency or simply enjoy the tranquility of nature, mastering various fishing techniques can be both rewarding and practical. This chapter explores different fishing methods, offering actionable advice for beginners and emphasizing the importance of ethical and sustainable practices.

Choosing the right fishing method depends on factors such as the type of water body, the species of fish you are targeting, and your personal preferences. One of the most common and accessible methods is rod and reel fishing. This technique is versatile and can be used in both freshwater and saltwater environments. For beginners, starting with a simple spinning reel and rod combo is ideal. These setups are easy to use and maintain, making them perfect for learning the basics.

Casting is a fundamental skill in rod and reel fishing. Proper casting technique involves holding the rod with a firm but relaxed grip, using the wrist to flick the rod tip forward, and releasing the line at the right moment to send the bait or lure into the water. Practice makes perfect, and spending time honing your casting skills will improve your accuracy and distance. Pay attention to the environment around you to avoid snagging your line on trees or other obstacles.

Selecting the right bait or lure is crucial for attracting fish. Live bait, such as worms, minnows, and insects, is often very effective because it mimics the natural food sources of fish. Artificial lures, on the other hand, come in various shapes, sizes, and colors designed to imitate prey and trigger a predatory response. Popular types of lures include spinners, jigs, and crankbaits. Experimenting with different baits and lures will help you determine what works best in your fishing area and for the species you are targeting.

Fly fishing is another popular technique that requires skill and practice. Unlike traditional rod and reel fishing, fly fishing uses a lightweight lure called a fly, which is typically made from feathers, fur, and other materials to imitate insects. The key to fly fishing is mastering the casting technique, which involves a fluid, rhythmic motion to cast the line and fly onto the water's surface. Fly fishing is particularly effective in rivers and streams where fish feed on insects.

Trolling is a technique often used in larger bodies of water, such as lakes and oceans. This method involves dragging baited lines or lures behind a moving boat. Trolling allows you to cover a large area and is effective for catching species such as salmon, trout, and walleye. The speed of the boat and the depth at which the bait or lure is presented are critical factors in successful trolling. Downriggers and planer boards can be used to control the depth and spread of your lines.

Ice fishing is a specialized technique practiced in cold climates where lakes freeze over. This method involves drilling holes in the ice and dropping baited lines into the water below. Ice fishing requires specific equipment, such as an ice auger to make holes, ice rods that are shorter and sturdier than traditional rods, and shelters to protect against the cold. Safety is paramount when ice fishing; always check the thickness of the ice and be aware of changing weather conditions.

For those who prefer a more passive approach, setline fishing can be effective. This technique involves setting lines with multiple hooks, baited and left unattended for a period. Setlines can be used in both freshwater and saltwater environments and are particularly useful for catching catfish, carp, and other bottom-dwelling species. When using setlines, it's important to mark them clearly and check them regularly to ensure caught fish are not left to suffer.

Another passive method is trapping, which involves using various types of traps and nets to catch fish. Fish traps, such as funnel traps and hoop nets, are designed to allow fish to enter but not exit. These traps can be placed in rivers, streams, and along shorelines to intercept fish moving through the area. Gill nets and seine nets are also commonly used to capture fish, especially in commercial fishing. When using traps and nets, it's essential to follow local regulations and practice sustainable fishing to avoid overharvesting.

Spear fishing is an ancient technique that requires skill and precision. This method involves using a spear or harpoon to catch fish, either from above the water or while diving. Spear fishing can be practiced in both freshwater and saltwater environments. For beginners, using a pole spear or Hawaiian sling can be a good starting point. This technique demands good aim and an understanding of fish behavior, as well as safety precautions when diving.

Regardless of the fishing method you choose, understanding fish behavior and habitat is crucial. Fish are influenced by various factors, including water temperature, weather conditions, and seasonal changes. For example, many fish species are more active during dawn and dusk, known as the "golden hours" of fishing. Additionally, fish often seek out specific structures, such as underwater vegetation, rocks, and drop-offs, where they can find food and shelter. Observing these patterns and adjusting your techniques accordingly will increase your chances of success.

Ethical fishing practices are essential for preserving fish populations and maintaining healthy ecosystems. Catch and release is a common practice that involves returning fish to the water after catching them, especially if they are undersized or not needed for consumption. When practicing catch and release, handle fish gently and minimize their time out of the water to reduce stress and injury. Using barbless hooks can also make it easier to release fish without causing harm.

Conservation efforts extend beyond individual practices. Supporting sustainable fisheries and respecting local regulations help protect fish populations for future generations. Many regions have established quotas, size limits, and seasonal restrictions to ensure the sustainability of fish stocks. By adhering to these regulations and advocating for responsible fishing practices, anglers can contribute to the long-term health of aquatic ecosystems.

Fishing is not only about catching fish but also about enjoying the experience and connecting with nature. Whether you are standing on a riverbank, casting from a boat, or sitting by an ice hole, fishing offers moments of tranquility and reflection. It provides an opportunity to observe wildlife, appreciate the beauty of natural landscapes, and unwind from the stresses of daily life. Sharing these experiences with family and friends can create lasting memories and foster a sense of community.

One memorable fishing trip might involve a serene morning on a lake, where the mist rises from the water's surface and the only sounds are the calls of birds and the gentle lapping of waves. As you cast your line and wait for a bite, you become attuned to the subtle rhythms of nature. The thrill of feeling a tug on the line and the excitement of reeling in a fish are moments of pure joy and satisfaction.

For those who pursue fishing as a way to enhance self-sufficiency, the skills and knowledge gained are invaluable. Knowing how to catch and prepare fish provides a reliable food source that can supplement other means of sustenance. Learning to clean and cook fish ensures that nothing goes to waste, and experimenting with different recipes can add variety to your diet.

In conclusion, fishing techniques encompass a wide range of methods that cater to different environments, target species, and personal preferences. By mastering the basics, understanding fish behavior, and practicing ethical fishing, you can enjoy a fulfilling and sustainable fishing experience. Whether you are a novice or an experienced angler, the journey of learning and improving your fishing skills offers endless opportunities for growth and connection with the natural world.

Food Preservation Methods

Preserving food has been a critical aspect of human survival for centuries, enabling people to extend the shelf life of their harvests and maintain a steady supply of nutrition through lean seasons. Mastering various food preservation methods is essential for anyone looking to enhance self-sufficiency and ensure food security. This chapter delves into traditional and modern techniques of food preservation, offering practical advice for beginners aiming to keep their food fresh and safe over extended periods.

One of the oldest and most reliable methods of preserving food is drying. By removing moisture, you create an inhospitable environment for bacteria, yeast, and mold, which rely on water to grow. Sun drying is an ancient technique that remains effective today. Thinly sliced fruits, vegetables, and herbs can be placed on racks or trays and left in the sun for several days until they are completely dehydrated. This method works best in hot, dry climates. For those living in more humid areas, using an oven or a food dehydrator provides a controlled environment to achieve the same results. Properly dried foods should be brittle or leathery and can be stored in airtight containers to prevent reabsorption of moisture.

Canning is another popular preservation method that involves placing foods in jars and heating them to a temperature that destroys microorganisms and inactivates enzymes. There are two main types of canning: water bath canning and pressure canning. Water bath canning is suitable for high-acid foods like fruits, pickles, and tomatoes. These foods are packed into jars, covered with boiling water, and processed for a specified time. Pressure canning, on the other hand, is necessary for low-acid foods such as vegetables, meats, and soups. These foods require higher temperatures than boiling water can provide, which is achieved using a pressure canner. Mastering canning requires attention to detail and adherence to safety guidelines to prevent the risk of botulism and other foodborne illnesses.

Freezing is a widely used preservation method that maintains the nutritional value, flavor, and texture of food. By lowering the temperature to below zero degrees Fahrenheit, the growth of microorganisms is halted, and enzyme activity is slowed significantly. Almost all types of food can be frozen, from fruits and vegetables to meats and prepared dishes. To freeze vegetables, blanching them first—briefly boiling them and then plunging them into ice water—helps preserve their color, texture, and flavor. Proper packaging is crucial to prevent freezer burn, which can occur when food is exposed to air. Using airtight containers or heavy-duty freezer bags and removing as much air as possible before sealing helps maintain the quality of frozen foods.

Fermentation is a natural preservation method that enhances the nutritional value and flavor of food. This process involves the conversion of sugars and carbohydrates into alcohol or organic acids by microorganisms such as yeast and bacteria.

Fermented foods, such as sauerkraut, kimchi, yogurt, and sourdough bread, are rich in probiotics, which are beneficial for gut health. To ferment vegetables, submerge them in a saltwater brine or mix them with salt to create their own brine, then leave them at room temperature to allow the beneficial bacteria to proliferate. Fermentation times vary, so tasting the food periodically helps determine when it has reached the desired flavor and texture.

Pickling is a preservation method that involves immersing food in an acidic solution, usually vinegar, which prevents the growth of spoilage-causing microorganisms. Pickled foods can range from cucumbers and onions to eggs and fish. The key to successful pickling is maintaining the correct balance of vinegar, water, salt, and spices. Quick pickling, or refrigerator pickling, is a simple method where food is packed into jars with a hot vinegar solution and stored in the refrigerator. These pickles are ready to eat in a few days and can last for several weeks. For longer-term storage, processing jars of pickled foods in a water bath canner ensures they are shelf-stable.

Smoking is a method that not only preserves food but also imparts a distinctive flavor. This technique involves exposing food to smoke from burning wood or other plant materials. There are two types of smoking: cold smoking and hot smoking. Cold smoking occurs at temperatures below 85 degrees Fahrenheit and is used primarily for flavoring rather than cooking. Foods such as cheese, nuts, and fish are common candidates for cold smoking. Hot smoking, which occurs at temperatures between 165 and 250 degrees Fahrenheit, both cooks and flavors the food. Meats, poultry, and fish are often hot smoked to achieve a tender, smoky result. Ensuring proper smoking times and temperatures is essential to prevent the growth of harmful bacteria.

Salting, or curing, is a method that involves using salt to draw moisture out of food, creating an environment inhospitable to bacteria. This technique has been used for centuries to preserve meats and fish. Dry curing involves rubbing salt, sometimes combined with sugar and spices, directly onto the food. Wet curing, or brining, involves soaking the food in a saltwater solution. The length of time required for curing depends on the size and type of food. After curing, storing the food in a cool, dry place extends its shelf life. Some cured foods, such as ham and bacon, may also be smoked for additional preservation and flavor.

Vacuum sealing is a modern preservation method that extends the shelf life of food by removing air and sealing it in airtight plastic bags. This method is particularly effective when combined with freezing or refrigeration. Vacuum sealing prevents the growth of aerobic bacteria and mold, which require oxygen to thrive. It also helps prevent freezer burn and preserves the flavor and texture of food. Vacuum sealers range from small, handheld devices to larger, countertop models, making this method accessible for home use.

Preservation with sugar, such as making jams, jellies, and preserves, involves cooking fruit with sugar to create a high-sugar environment that inhibits microbial growth. Pectin, a natural gelling agent found in fruit, is often added to achieve the desired consistency. The mixture is cooked until it reaches the appropriate thickness, then poured into sterilized jars and sealed. Properly made and sealed jams and jellies can be stored at room temperature for up to a year. This method not only preserves the fruit but also concentrates its flavors, making it a delicious addition to your pantry.

Root cellaring is a traditional method that utilizes the natural cool, humid conditions of an underground cellar to store root vegetables, fruits, and other perishables. A root cellar can be as simple as a cool basement or a dedicated underground structure. The key is maintaining a stable temperature and humidity level to prevent spoilage and dehydration. Root cellars are ideal for storing potatoes, carrots, apples, and other produce that benefits from a cool, dark environment. Proper ventilation and periodic inspection of stored items help ensure long-term preservation.

Learning and applying these food preservation methods can significantly enhance your self-sufficiency and reduce food waste. Each technique offers unique benefits and challenges, and mastering them requires practice and attention to detail. By diversifying your preservation methods, you can enjoy a variety of foods year-round, even when they are out of season. Moreover, preserving your own food allows you to control the ingredients and avoid preservatives and additives found in many commercially processed foods.

Food preservation is a skill that connects us to our ancestors and the rhythms of nature. Whether you are drying herbs from your garden, canning the summer's bounty of tomatoes, or fermenting vegetables into tangy pickles, each method carries with it a sense of tradition and resourcefulness. The satisfaction of opening a jar of home-preserved peaches in the middle of winter or sharing a slice of homemade smoked ham with loved ones is immeasurable.

In the journey toward self-sufficiency, understanding and implementing various food preservation techniques is a cornerstone. It empowers you to make the most of your harvests, reduce dependency on store-bought goods, and ensure that you and your family have access to nutritious, flavorful food throughout the year. As you experiment with these methods, you will develop a deeper appreciation for the food you grow and the effort required to preserve it, fostering a more sustainable and fulfilling way of living.

Building a Food Storage System

Organizing a reliable food storage system is a fundamental step towards achieving self-sufficiency and ensuring you and your family have an adequate supply of food during times of need. Whether you're preparing for emergencies, aiming to reduce waste, or simply want to make the most of your harvest, a well-thought-out food storage system is essential.

The first step in building an effective food storage system is assessing your needs. Consider the size of your household, dietary preferences, and the types of food you consume regularly. Take into account any special dietary requirements, such as allergies or medical conditions, that may necessitate storing specific types of food. Once you have a clear understanding of your needs, you can begin to plan the types and quantities of food to store.

A successful food storage system incorporates a variety of food types to ensure nutritional balance. Staples such as grains, legumes, and pasta provide a foundation of carbohydrates and proteins. Including a mix of canned and dried fruits and vegetables ensures access to essential vitamins and minerals. Proteins can be stored in the form of canned meats, fish, and beans, while fats can be sourced from items like cooking oils, nuts, and seeds. Don't forget to include comfort foods and treats, which can provide emotional support during challenging times.

Proper organization is key to maintaining an efficient food storage system. Designate a specific area in your home for food storage, whether it's a pantry, basement, or dedicated room. Ensure the space is cool, dry, and dark, as these conditions help prolong the shelf life of stored foods. Arrange your food items in a logical order, with frequently used items easily accessible and less frequently used items stored further back. Use shelves, bins, and labels to keep everything organized and easy to find.

Rotation is a critical aspect of maintaining a food storage system. Adopt the "first in, first out" (FIFO) method, where you use the oldest items first to ensure nothing goes to waste. Regularly check expiration dates and inspect stored food for signs of spoilage, such as unusual odors, discoloration, or signs of pests. Make it a habit to incorporate stored food into your daily meals, replacing what you use to keep your supply fresh and up-to-date.

Water storage is an often overlooked but vital component of a comprehensive food storage system. Each person in your household should have a minimum of one gallon of water per day for drinking and sanitation purposes. Store water in food-grade containers, and consider having both bottled water and larger containers for long-term storage. To ensure water quality, rotate stored water every six months and consider using water purification methods such as filters, purification tablets, or boiling.

Investing in proper storage containers can significantly extend the shelf life of your food. Airtight containers protect against moisture, pests, and air exposure, which can cause spoilage. Mylar bags, vacuum-sealed bags, and food-grade buckets with gamma lids are excellent choices for long-term storage. For dry goods like grains and legumes, adding oxygen absorbers to the containers can help prevent oxidation and extend shelf life.

In addition to storing food, consider preserving your own. Home canning, dehydrating, and freezing are excellent ways to extend the life of your homegrown produce and reduce dependency on store-bought items. Learning these skills not only enhances your food storage system but also provides a rewarding way to enjoy the fruits of your labor year-round.

Building a food storage system is not just about stockpiling food; it's about creating a sustainable cycle of consumption and replenishment. Regularly review and update your inventory, adjusting quantities based on your family's changing needs. Stay informed about shelf life and storage conditions for different types of food to ensure you're maximizing their longevity.

Maintaining a detailed inventory is essential for keeping track of your food storage. Use a spreadsheet, notebook, or digital app to record the types and quantities of food you have, along with their expiration dates. This will help you manage your stock, plan meals, and identify what needs to be replenished. Regularly updating your inventory ensures you are always aware of what you have on hand and can make informed decisions about what to use next.

Consider the practicalities of accessing your stored food during an emergency. Having a plan for how you will retrieve and prepare food without access to electricity or running water is crucial. Store manual can openers, portable stoves, and sufficient fuel sources alongside your food supplies. Practice using these tools and cooking methods to ensure you are prepared to use them when needed.

Community can play a significant role in building and maintaining a food storage system. Engaging with neighbors, friends, and local organizations can provide valuable support and resources. Consider joining or forming a local food storage group where members can share knowledge, exchange surplus items, and support each other in times of need. Community gardens and co-ops are also excellent ways to supplement your food storage with fresh produce and locally sourced items.

Education is an ongoing part of maintaining a food storage system. Stay informed about best practices for food storage, preservation techniques, and emergency preparedness. Books, online courses, and local workshops can provide valuable knowledge and skills. Sharing what you learn with family members ensures everyone is prepared and can contribute to maintaining the system.

Financial planning is an integral aspect of building a food storage system. Budgeting for the initial investment in supplies and ongoing replenishment helps ensure your system is sustainable. Look for sales, bulk purchasing options, and discounts to make the most of your budget. Remember that investing in a food storage system is an investment in your family's security and well-being.

Sustainability should be a guiding principle as you develop your food storage system. Aim to minimize waste by using what you store and storing what you use. Composting food scraps and expired items can reduce waste and contribute to your garden's fertility. Choosing reusable and recyclable storage containers also supports a sustainable approach.

Psychological preparedness is an often underestimated aspect of emergency planning. Knowing you have a well-stocked food storage system can provide peace of mind and reduce anxiety during uncertain times. Involving family members in planning, organizing, and maintaining the system fosters a sense of shared responsibility and preparedness.

Building a food storage system is a dynamic process that evolves with your family's needs and circumstances. Regularly reviewing and adjusting your approach ensures it remains effective and relevant. Embrace the journey of learning and adapting as you work towards a resilient and self-sufficient lifestyle.

In conclusion, a well-organized food storage system is a cornerstone of self-sufficiency and emergency preparedness. By assessing your needs, organizing your supplies, maintaining proper storage conditions, and staying informed, you can create a system that provides security and peace of mind. Engaging with your community, continually educating yourself, and adopting sustainable practices further enhance the effectiveness of your food storage efforts. With careful planning and commitment, you can ensure that your family has access to nutritious, safe, and delicious food, no matter what challenges may arise.

Printed in the USA
CPSIA information can be obtained
at www.ICGtesting.com
CBHW071824300724
12432CB00025B/676